Every Shameless Ray

Copyright © 2018 Leslie Timmins

Except for the use of short passages for review purposes, no part of this book may be reproduced, in part or in whole, or transmitted in any form or by any means, electronically or mechanically, including photocopying, recording, or any information or storage retrieval system, without prior permission in writing from the publisher.

 Canada Council for the Arts   Conseil des Arts du Canada

The publisher gratefully acknowledges the support of the Canada Council for the Arts and the Ontario Arts Council for its publishing program. The publisher is also grateful for the financial assistance received from the Government of Canada.

Front cover artwork: Leslie Timmins, "Signal," multimedia, 28 cm x 35.5 cm, copyright ©2016, 2018

Front cover design: Celia Jong

Library and Archives Canada Cataloguing in Publication

Timmins, Leslie, 1955-, author
    Every shameless ray / Leslie Timmins.

(Inanna poetry & fiction series)
Poems.
ISBN 978-1-77133-577-5 (softcover)

    I. Title. II. Series: Inanna poetry and fiction series

PS8639.I565E94 2018   C811'.6   C2018-904382-2

Printed and bound in Canada

Inanna Publications and Education Inc.
210 Founders College, York University
4700 Keele Street, Toronto, Ontario M3J 1P3 Canada
Telephone: (416) 736–5356 Fax (416) 736–5765
Email: inanna.publications@inanna.ca Website: www.inanna.ca

 MIX
Paper from responsible sources
FSC   FSC® C004071

Every Shameless Ray

POEMS BY
LESLIE TIMMINS

inanna poetry & fiction series

INANNA Publications and Education Inc.
Toronto, Canada

for Ron Grant

Contents

THE CALLING

Anatta (What Can't Be Searched For)	3
Flight of the Undertaker Bee	4
Connor, East Third Avenue	6
Reincarnation of the Horse as Lover	7
The Field Speaks of its Persistence	8
Caul	10
You Can't Help but Love	12
The Winter Boys	14
The Stoning	15
Embedded: A Photograph of War	16
Triolet for Afghanistan	17
How I Have Come to This Country	18
Anaconda	19
Theory of Search and Find	20
Letters Home	21
The Prevailing Wind	23
I Have Taken to the Earth Today	25
Plot	27
The Calling	28

ECHO

I Saw My Mother's Face the Day I Was Born	31

Sibyl of Delphi, Sistine Chapel	32
A Place Like This	34
The Long Nerve	36
Dear Cancer	38
Flash	61
In the Meditation Hall	63
How the Heart Grows Strong Again	64
The Batter	66
Burning Through	67
From Jericho Pier	69
Lives of the Soul	70
What is Served	71

A FINE DISORDER

On Encountering *Bonheur de Vivre* by Matisse	75
In the Morning When They Fling the Shutters Wide	76
From That Night a Fine Disorder	78
The Conversation	79
Even If It Isn't There	81
Shadow, 1905	83
When Lightning Strikes Only Colours Burn	84
Witness: Artist and Model	85
The Limits of Windows	86
Transit	87
Slice, *The Piano Lesson,* 1916	88
Jumble, 1917	89
Tilt	91

Woman Before Woman Before a Fish Bowl, 1922	92
Henriette	93
Seated Woman, Back Turned	94
Uncaged, 1948	95
Calling like Prayer (Chapel of the Rosary, 1951)	96
Henriette Darricarrére	97
The First Supper	99
Notes on the Poems	101
Acknowledgements	104

*But the sun
underfoot is so dazzling
down there among the sundews,
there is so much light
in that cup that, looking,
you start to fall upward.*
—Amy Clampitt

The heart is the smaller cousin of the sun.
—Joy Harjo

Luminous, monks, is the mind.
—Guatama Buddha

The Calling

Anatta (What Can't Be Searched For)*

When the pack horses carrying you to your gold rush
grow gaunt, buck off their burden, and desert you,
even your enemy is lost.
Then the road you shunned comes round again
and you unravel like a tapestry of cloth.

Soldier Beggar Lover Saviour — all the figures
you've woven to keep yourself together
strip back to the quiet
in the loom's wooden combs

and how long has it been here?
the gold you've ached for limned
in the spaces
between the loosed threads

anatta

the spinning tale unspun

what can't be searched for
is found.

Anatta (an-atta) is a Buddhist term for the non-existence of an abiding self as the core characteristic of existence is impermanence.

Flight of the Undertaker Bee

for Connor

I don't want to hear
        about the bees that wait
              for the corpse
to dry, lighten up in the hallway
        of the hive
               so they can carry it
high, unusually high
        into the tops
              of trees so they can drop it.

Tell me about the Cheezie
        you put in the spirit house
              with its tiny shingles and eaves.
Like a brown-brown
        birdhouse with that bright orange
              weird-power
offering to keep bad things
        away. You tell me
not to say *penis* when the killer
        whale swims by the window at the aquarium.
Penis? I say
        Now the dog gets the Cheezie
and the spirits can get me
        any old day.

You tell me bees swarm

       when they're happy,
huddle up
       when they're cold
dance in the dark
       to show where the sun went.
In the intricate
       waxy
hallways
       of your hive, there are no private parts,
so where is the sting?

       Even with five eyes, you tell me,
bees can't see the true
       colour of the rose.

Connor, East Third Avenue

On our way
                to the store you bend

all the way over,
                            pull

your jacket up
                      I think you're going to moon me

dis me with a six-year-old's
                    disdain

—an hour at the table,
                  the *wrong* ketchup, *sour* bread—

but you only want a scratch
                        Slow,

please
            up the ghost-thin

doorknobs of your spine,
                          sticks of wings

crouching under fledgling
                      skin.

Reincarnation of the Horse as Lover

(*I pushed my baby sister*
along the old road in the pasture
in a black buggy, he said

And she, I asked, *how small was she?*
  Oh, small, he said,
And white, her skin, very white?
  Yes, I remember)

In the same pasture his horse (best friend)
grazed
the one who walked backwards fastest
and won him a ribbon,
and the dog who died a yellow patch over one eye
under a late harvest blade

I did not say   care for me
the way you cared for   the horse
                          dog
                          sister

but on the path in the growing field, the grass worn low
where I've been swimming and drowning
backwards and forwards all this time looking
for you, I want to say (I *almost* say) *Leave them,*
Come home to me, but the bullet for the horse sings
under my feet (echoes and sings) until I am far enough away.

The Field Speaks of its Persistence

I know, too,
That the blackbird is involved
In what I know.
—Wallace Stevens

you drive through me your windows open radio on
the horses along the fence watch you
and the grasslands east and west

early morning light's playing with matter

electrons bound off the metal hood of the car atoms
entangle superconduct flux the order of the day
on the ridge a poplar strips its branches down to

the velvet of antlers its trunk a pivot black hinge

black bird that swims out of itself and back in so close
to your windshield you're forced   to slow down   tune-out
your radio pull-over and shaking lean

on a fence post where the horses' great heads hang deep

in thought memories of leather traces eased furrowed fields
salt-licks as a mare looks up meets your eye
it lasts just a second

that glimpse of how light slows

the mare's memories quickening now through your brain
all of your feet heavy as stone
having passed through walls skin your elation

will turn to confusion how you'll know when

it happens again but for now
it's bliss all along
you've belonged here

across the fence the car idles
its radio kicking in
and out

Caul

I tip my kayak and roll,
hanging like a dancer in a sac of light.

The boat is meant for this. It rolls easily
onto its belly and waits above me like a friend.

There's another woman in the pool tonight.
Her man stands in the water beside her.

His hands are on her boat.

I wanted this so much — just to flip my kayak and swing back up

Underwater, the pool-light flickers blue.
I can see the flat density of trapezius over scapula,
a deltoid curve. I am as if I am swimming behind myself.

I swing my paddle hard in an arc like the sun,
drive my left knee against the inside of the hull and flick my hip,
once —

I'm *up*, streaming
water loud off the back
of my head —

                        so elk-calves swim
                        within hours of birth
                        from island to riverbank

                              we slap paddles into down-currents,

revolve
upside-down
and travel like that

through hollow rooms of the river,
pass drowning trees, slip
into quick-streams, skim
slack.
In head-splitting cold,
righten.

Soon we'll be lonely.
Our marrows ache to fly through the green channel.

No bones to name us. No doors.

You Can't Help but Love

Explain the hours spent
with a borrowed paddle
in your living room,
planting it flat on the coffee table to spin
into the spume & spray
of the gold shag rug.

In the rapids outside town
when you plant your paddle
flat on a boulder
and spin *Yee-Haa!* into the tow of the river,
your new skill ensures you aren't sucked
into the sink-hole
that could drag you along the riverbed
and spit you out maybe
somewhere downstream

and you look over to see your teacher watch you spin away,
shake his head, call it a *fluke*.

In your medicine pouch there's nothing to help you
not-care what he thinks,
and you can't help but love how he looks,
the ridge of muscle along his thigh,

the glide of his boat near the top of the Falls
that flies your fancy out to Realms of Mist & Roar,
but he can't bear you looking at him.

In bed at night, the river comes to you,
ripples your spine, puts you back in the current.

The Winter Boys

All the way up to Brandywine Meadows we were looking for summer,
late-June, climbing under hemlocks dripping mist,
bushwhacking through salal and mud flecked with cone,
until we spit out at an evergreen edge into a field of snow.

Sun-blind, out-of-season, but still searching for what isn't here,
plumes of pink fireweed and green meadows,
not this bowl of snow sunk in a round of peaks
and bare-chested boys on snowmobiles
riding high in an avalanche chute.

One stands below the ramparts, girds his machine upward with his feet,
flicks hand-gears to spin, almost freefall down through the chute
over bones of saplings and young mountain goats,
down to the verge of a frozen creek, where he swerves, exhales,
the skin of his chest dazzling, a sun-blade as he whirs away.

Under the snow, the crackle of seeds and trickle of creek,
the land in its late beauty breathing,
what we'd called summer, a narrative of ascent,
is our breath within that breathing.

The Stoning

(*after* The Stoning, *a collage by Perry Fletcher Thompson*)

If you enter here
a scarlet sky will ache behind you
like a vast flag or wound about to be struck
by the men standing before it, bent
at ardent angle to take aim,
force open at chest and groin, a figure who crouches
in the foreground,
like the snow beneath the men senseless
to their violence as to their beauty,
the sky behind them
already bloody, each playing his part,
all silent and moving, but one.

All silent and moving, but one
already bloody, each playing his part,
the sky behind them
violent to their beauty
like the snow beneath them senseless,
and in the foreground,
forced open at chest and groin, a figure who crouches
at ardent angle to take aim
at the men standing before him, bent
like a vast flag or wound about to be struck,
the scarlet sky aching behind them
if you enter here.

Embedded: A Photograph of War

The man's head is bagged tied at the neck and the child he presses to
        his side though open-eyed and bare-headed is no
less bound Inside razor-wire on yellow sand a small boy cries beside a
        blind man Whose hand nevertheless caresses the
boy's forehead Whose white tunic nevertheless brightens twisted barbs
        and over-lapping coil Which make this a prize-
winner and the caption written by the famous photographer praising
        the mercy of the imprisoning army Which allows
him to travel in their corps Which lets a dad and his kid stick together
        Which nevertheless places a hood over the dad's
head Which without irony is beautifully captured shining in stifling
        seatcover-pleather That nevertheless makes us
all children and travellers to the same oasis where only an enemy's
        embrace gives and takes away the taste we thirst for.

Triolet for Afghanistan

> *my country*
> *is a fractured mirror*
> *a continuous fire*
> *a burning garden*
> —Asadulla Habib

At Kag Khana four boys flee
the peacekeepers' war, the Pashtun lords.
Sandflies tear their cheeks, scars seed
at Kag Khana. Four boys flee
across mountains bereft of the grace of trees
that will cast them back
to Kag Khana four shadows to be
peacekeepers, lords of war?

How I Have Come to This Country

I have found you, beloved,
        shining without trying
where I never would have looked
        scarred, unhooked
never would have known a man like you
        slip skin from the fruit
spoon aside tallow pulp scoop-out
        fragrant first seeds
then find another, lower row,
        second chance of wet black beads
peppering the sweet where only suns
        had tongued before.
A man, you, who knows the heart's
        dark ripening.

Anaconda

Gone are the cities and the sun.
The thunder's in the long grass.
                —Tomas Tranströmer

In the passageway, every door tried,
every room entered is a skin
looking for a fit.
To know what is needed,
what might be mine.

Where I came from, there was no room
to belong in. The blade,
always poised,

yet here you are, Anaconda,
the slow wind of your coils wave-like
into the very heart of my house,
your scales filigreed in gold leaf and jaws
monstrous that we might have
killed with, but for the knowing
in the back of my brain
this was not to be my way.

Your gold confirms the good again,
that I have landed in the long grass,
in the rivers you swim in, the rivers I am.

Theory of Search and Find

I've lived too long where I can be reached.
                                   —Rumi

If we could suspend ourselves in stillness
over the earth's hot dancing

line a room with metal, suck all of the air
out, then squeeze light

itself to lower the high and raise the low
frequencies, even quantum noise

that tiny random jitterbug racket
would quiet

and we would hear the murmurations of gravity
rippling in space

and wouldn't it be just like us
to make such an effort

rapt in our own stillness and still
not know what holds us here.

Letters Home

—for RG

From the wooden bridge
the carp looks frozen,
suspended in mire.
If I could scrape the cloud away
would its crimson heart flower?

In this clearing grey soldiers gather as pines, their branches too high,
too few to ease their loneliness, the spaces between them reflecting

only the spaces between them

(if pines could gather in soldiers,
a company could keep?)

Today even you, my love, are your own army, a crooked bone, your
thoughts those clouds above the hemlocks,

who can say?

Brittle ice draws the maple leaves
scissor-sharp below.
Even now I can't say
how to free them
without hurting myself.

You, my love, exist in a space beside me when once you slipped

round me blissfully fitting, your hand reaching for mine in sleep,
your heat—forgive me, I went away

fell from the light above the canopy of trees and can't touch
that ache, today a soldier finding home in these letters I write.

The Prevailing Wind

An eagle liquid as a manta ray swims
the visible shallows of wind,
the tallest trees shake, branches bounce
as we breathe it in and our ribs unlace,
our flesh, so easily, wing.

The random springing of green at the tips of leaves,
the littoral forest we live within,
in separate rooms or tangled in our bed,
you overworked, buried in a book,
me remembering a dream of fumbling
with my bridal gown
as something unknown waits.

Eager to shake off that fear,
I ask you to walk down the hill to the sea,
but you surprise me, *Don't ask
because I'll want to please you,* and you're crying,
much more tired than I knew
and I hold you wondering
at the shape of things.

Down the hill late in the day
I arrive at a blasted beach, fury in the sea,
my hood drenched in seconds, umbrella inside-out.
I want to look south but the wind won't let me,
it's behind my knees howling,

unfurling waves to white,
my face feels raw, exhilarated—*Mild Peril*
as the censor warns at the beginning of the movie,
but we are nowhere near the beginning.

My flashlight-beam glances off the mud road,
the diamond-wet leaves. I switch it off,
tune in to the wood's early darkness;
the sound of the surf recedes as the road rises,
the hill you said would kill you today, kill
your mending heart,
when sudden, bright,
your headlights blaze towards me.

I Have Taken to the Earth Today

We make love before, knowing
we'll be tired,
and we dance right to the end
say good-bye, pay the waiters
and drive home, 4 a.m.,
stay awhile in the empty street,
so full of gladness we stand a little apart,
sway

cats join us, step from under bushes
into the crossroads,
sit near one another
without territory or rush
as if patient for the slow-coming dawn.

You go in, I stay here on the lawn
swinging my gold wedding
shoes from my hands.
The sky still, square of lawn tipped
to the curve of Earth,
five crows flying over me,
four more within arms' reach,
serrated wing-beats, then silence
after that almost-enterable world.

Just an hour with wings, what
trouble could it cause?
Then the stain of lobelia in the terracotta pot,
the trunks of the cedars, like sentries,
and out of the east a waking wind to shake the boughs,
their mesmerizing sway.

Plot

A summer night heat in the cracks of the sidewalks
for coolness my love and I pack in with the others
to the old movie-house on Broadway and when the lights
come down and the movie starts we see the door
of the projection room has been left open
the projectionist asleep or out to get a cold one
and on the screen the door's reflection no one
stands or calls out to whoever has left us
to our own devices finding the stills in the rush
of light and shadow
working that door into the plot.

The Calling

There is a bird
that calls three
times the same,
sustains
a little longer the last note,
and calls again.

This morning the wind
has the voice
of a delicate threshing machine,
the acacias stretch out their branches
in streams
to be caressed
by a calling

that the maples toss
their scarlet leaves up
into and over as sunlight
bends through the window-glass, heats
my ear and my shoulder.

Echo

I Saw My Mother's Face the Day I Was Born

I saw my mother's face the day I was born
hushed with an unbelieving surprise at what she had done
—tiny and complete, staring up at her jaw
and the slow way she turned her head
to see me again—
moving, alight in her arms.

Lost forty years, the memory streams black-and-white jumpy
as an old home movie, as if I hadn't made
this other mother and between my breasts
tend and cradle her who never
forgot what she could do.

Sibyl of Delphi, Sistine Chapel

I lay on my back on a slivery pew and pretended to feel faint.
It was hot, there'd been beggars, my first, on the road
to the Sistine waving waxy stumps and widows in black,
grave-faced, making their way to Vespers. My mother knelt,
my father said, Popes were Generals then and killed
and warred, my sister stuck by the Pietà.

I know Michelangelo gave you, Sibyl, the same body
he gives everyone,
never far from stone, the quarry at Carrera,
but when I was ten years old, your lime-and-mandarin robe
flowing over arms like plinths and the ham-fist
that pinched your cape, were unremarkable.

Rosaries clicked, a tour of nuns, swish of black habits,
my mother regretting her conversion by mere Protestants,
my father regretting nothing, my sister, lost;
from the ceiling, Sibyl, you watched us all,

your eyes' roundness conveyed your attendance
to the harrying voices of gods, and cherubs,
infants with the thighs of men,
conferring like priests over your prophecies.

A scud of wind, your hair outstretched,
you listened to voices that split the air like adzes,
stuttered or limped towards you,

we futurists, children, knaves yearning
for you to open the quarry, let us out,
so tenderly you listened,
the sweetness of your face
above your body's brutal shape.

A Place Like This

High above the mud flats of a bay
these hills hide fields of lavender
where dragonflies like box-kites bump
into me, a scarecrow in this place.

The sound of nickering draws me down
from the fields to a barn's open doors,
where feeding sacks hang from a rafter
and just outside and below, blind-folded horses

canter and buck round a corral.
A brindled gelding and chestnut mare slow
into the shade of trees,
one long neck resting over another,
not sightless after all, but netted against flies

as their secret eyes look out and their nares quiver,
sawdust sweet from new alder posts
and from the fields lavender.
I haven't heard what the Tarot will tell

at the booth up the hill when the revels begin.
I haven't seen the woman who'll look through me
as if I were a window from crown to coccyx,
say, old sorrows hang heavily in you

but she didn't see the small girl running
headlong down the path until

she saw me, stumbled, then beamed
as if she were my own,

the child I couldn't keep
now steadied by another's hand.
In a place like this, she could even be me
when I had no mother at all

but galloped down paths wildly pleased.
She looks back at me
long after I climb the hill,
her eyes like reins, guiding.

The Long Nerve

In pink meat
pressed and packed
in a can a tiny
circle of bone sits
sudden as a tooth,
its centre pierced,
a dark tchick of sound,
the hole where the fight runs.

I pick the bone up, look
through and find
it's a segment
of spinal column still strung
somehow together,
each disk brusque,
crevicled,
a void staring out.

Under a cold tap
the segments split,
but when I lay each bone
on a black lacquer dish
they roll back
into their cord,
their scent brining
searching the air
like a mind sensing

for the body it left behind,
the long nerve
braided river
that carries you back
to the salt-stung
hunger of heart.

Dear Cancer

I.

The wind plays with the sea

making impressions of animals
at large underneath, as my body

breathes, makes its claim
on the stream of being

until a single word repeats   *metastases*

    metastases

and a portcullis plunges into the earth
its chains running

2.

Dear Cancer hear

the woman next to me
wheeled in after 7 hours of surgery
her 27th surgery

(*I will not forget you O my darling*)

she knows you too,
in the darkness the wound,
shunt gate we're trying to
hoist drag up
as we watch the wind for another

prophecy

3.

the wind crosses the sea
between our island
and the mainland as a series of winds
an intricacy of powers
neither driving
nor leading.

But I haven't told them
about the horses

crated   their haunches cramped
in a low stable shag-blind
half-starved
How could I forget you I cry
in dream after dream.

4.

When they found
the second cancer

I abandoned their bony postures
even the one who walked

when I asked her
on a swollen hock

who raced me
through the Schwarzwald

a wild child hunting
wild boar

5.

loyal animal if I get
back in the saddle

will you ride me to sun
rise or sun set?

6.

You stood by my hospital bed and willed me to breathe—
an excess of morphine   foolish self-administered-drip
your wordless intelligence reaching me: *husband*

Steel table, bucket, the unlovely taking

of the bride from her body
agreed to signed for evisceration of flesh-
orchids   sweet-girl-parts

and all the while you waited

just outside, nothing lost
between us.

7.

You who'd lived like a hurricane
furious against the slow accident of love
had learned to be this lonely,
to let the sound of birds over the inlet
lift your ship's anchor, unchain the sea,
reveal me to you.

8.

Then I, too, was in the frequency of birds,
the Golden Eye's piercing cry in the recovery room
as it startled up, skimmed out
over the other sleeping ships,
their anchors tight against their bows
and grey waves scaling
as the mind woke up
to find itself drowning.

9.

In panic, the body's a sorrowing weight
that drops into waves, drags behind
on a long forgotten chain

10.

(Dear Cancer,

in the mirror I saw you standing,
my shorn hair in your hands,
                    you unlock me.

I have tried with my knife to find you,
I have pulled my gates shut,
but all the dark strangers inside.)

11.

I shiver in my chair, dutifully recovering,
dutifully listening to an eagle call

a high, rapid shard imperatively repeating
as others climb thermals over the sea,
float, stall, ignoring her   hidden

in the thicket of trees below the house,
locating herself   *here, here!*

12.

I map myself onto the landscape:
one of millions and alone,

a woman on an island on a hill—
when under my chair the plush cat grunts

a hummer spikes inches from my eye,
cracks an electric whip

and flowers in the pea-vines let down
bitter seeds and nectaries.

13.

When I hear the eagle call again,
it's not stranded but part of another

treble call that crosses-over and splits
notes so finely I'm not sure

he wasn't there before,
her mate—something—calling back,

all day knowing
exactly where she was.

14.

We've seen them near here,
the killer whales in Trincomali
which are the sea describing itself as music, as skin.

A glossy black ridge carves up—
glimpse of white eye-patch, dorsal arc—
and then another whale glides into the side-stream
of the first, then another mother, brother, calf,
fins and tail-flukes making archways in the bodies
of their kin and descend in sequence
as a visible music.

15.

They know what they are, they speak it this way,
force-field   muscle   wild
hope we could be like them
one and many in the body of the sea,
step back in as they did, follow the salmon-run,
an unbroken blue *vibrato* in the memory of the whale
lost to our senses, but not perished.

16.

Some nights still
I climb in and out of graves

carry a limp Scottie dog and shake hands with the dead who
it has to be said, look a lot like me though their names

engrave a strange alphabet
on my hands.

17.

Some nights I stand in front of windows and tear
curtains apart, first the velvet, the sheers

then the pilled, stained sheets
right up through the middle and finally to glass

so I may see what's ahead,
diagnosis, how long I'll last.

18.

You know how it is,
how sometimes in the distance

there's a hunched hut and beyond it another
and doors that face away or perhaps there are no doors

and then I remember the Scottie dog—clownish, fearless,
loyal—have I *betrayed* myself?

one iffy blood-test and I make
my bed in the ragged earth

mainlining fear woozy
evidence of nothing much?

19.

So many ways to die this side of the grave
while the great herds roam through the ground-cloud

in the reach between the river that floods and dries up
where clearcuts on the mountains only look like an answer

and bears sleep long, deep
under warm snow.

20.

Here the land points to its own end
and the sea begins

Here we walk through upswells
of brome and early hairgrass

leaves the deer favour
and flowers they don't

growing white in the salted spray
as the last sea-lion slips

off a faraway rock into the boil of the sea
and the sky shuts down crimson-violet-ash

a sudden pressure wave-upon-
wave without pity

21.

In this enormity
the land's a thinning horn

then the deer step out of the dwarf trees
and walk round us carefully

out of the brome and early hairgrass
in twos and threes so close

we grasp each other's hand,
someone's earned their trust

let them graze the edge of their certainties
as they graze ours.

22.

And there they are
just under the surface of the water

full of the meat of the body   taut and silver
liquid with grace

what I asked for
when I asked to feel again

my own breath.
In the quiet of the night

you beside me dreaming
I attend to the cathedral

of my body's scarred
and saddened walls

and what I thought scarce
even vanished

swims beside me
salmon-skinned shark-finned

intent on feeding
whatever comes their way

and I don't run to the thinning shore
but stand among them breathing,

and when still I can't sleep
I think of all

the sleepless others
stepping in beside me.

Flash

The clerk has a beautiful brown V
of a widow's peak on her forehead
as she shows me, innocently,
how *it's all about layering this Fall,*
T-shirt under sweater under scarf.
Does it open in the front, I ask, fiddling,
Can I get it off fast?

The small of my back prickles a warning of coming heat,
and I squeeze into the change room
as my spine begins to drown its garden of fine hairs
and my cheeks, both pairs, flush.

I strip off my bra, peel my jeans to my knees
and stand there flashing, half-naked,
thinking, now, of you:

On another shopping trip,
carrying your try-on's rack-to-sweltering-rack,
peeling off my layers to find a gift,
and this morning under your new birthday shirt,
your cock so proud,
jeans flung on the bed
and our embrace at its edge brief,
no time before work to stroke, fondle, laugh,
but the sight of your sweet balls caught up
like a breath.

I walk home from the store empty-handed

along streets rose-red, apple-yellow with leaf.
Flash, love this world. *Flash,* hate it.
On our night table a tumbler of ice,
on our night table large and larger tubes of lube.

Nothing to hold onto, nothing stays still,
but somehow—how? still eager,
my own darling innards eager—

not as often and too hot or chill
but still wanting to climb rose-red, apple-yellow
and catch, be caught by you.

In the Meditation Hall

—for Michele McDonald

in this late winter afternoon
meditation hour,
as if I've been clearing a table
admiring the bowls of spoons
the fine intervals between tines
while through a night-window the sky sweeps
dazzling clear,
it flips

what was outside
is suddenly within

only the frame of the window remains
now ledged with the dust and shimmer of galaxies
shot through and far beyond
with a streaming sapphire-blue blackness

wow wow   the bliss flows in and out
  the door of the mind ajar   what shelter is this
framed and boundless   the innocent bliss tenderly
returning   *wow wow*   tenderly let go
the in-breath rising   in the intervals   between stars
        the small frame   the large
          tenderly   tenderly

How the Heart Grows Strong Again

I wake in the night as if summoned,
stumble to the table, pick up a book by Braasch
which opens to a photograph of alders
shot low with the dawn behind them
like the bent bars of a luminous jailhouse
and between them I can see the tree that woke me
traced like a map of old journeys worn through.

Streaming through tassels of moss-covered trunks
the sunlight makes and unmakes the illusion of its branches,
the reticulate veins of its leaves that cast
the solidity of the alders into doubt,
its transparency traced
like a map of old journeys worn through
and between them I can see the tree that woke me.

I know when I'm lost
I should take any road the land offers
from the end of love to whatever comes after,
but for this angel to appear calling
carrying my soul back from safekeeping
how can this be believed,
until I sleep, sound again.

Yet something hidden loves me
weeps at my thinness

feeds me tree-light
and wakes me all summer
from one thing and another
until I sleep, sound again,
how can this be believed.

The Batter

She stands at home, knees deep, feet planted wide
in a batter's stance,
and when she swings
the crack of the bat and snap of the ball are one elation

and when her thighs grip and she springs away,
her hands rise to catch
the full and heavy swing of her breasts
held against her as she sprints
in a natural balancing act
as the men step back
back
into the field, the crowd cheers,
and she seeks and wins the first base.

Burning Through

—for Bibiana Tomasic

      Dear friend
the woods smell drunk
    tonight
        at last light we walk through
        them
        sipping.

    Winter sap on the pine-
        bark's as piercing sweet
            as summer-mead
      to you and above
           the bare trees you drink-
in raven's black sails her
        wind-carved
        word.

            The skin of your throat's
      still   raw
from radiation but you
            stumble
        through the half-
      light eagerly the beat
        of energy you've
        seen
    streaming
            from your hands
into eternity

                    is this lightning-fired
                              tree springwood
                              winterwood
            burnt-   through
each ring thermo—
      thermo-dy-*namic*ally true—
            nothing lost   gained
            unlocked
                              merely
                to the spin
of planets ringing
now   in the *incar-*
            inc*ar*nadine
      west

            but
                  you
      Pilgrim
      Initiate   Friend shine
here not
            in eternity—
            drunken fools!— *here*
            where your
      eyes dishevel grin   mere
atoms and matter *no matter!*
                  still atom-*ic*-ally bound
            not immortal As-traea the star-
      maiden stuck in
         the-glory-
                  stars but *here* with me
               in the quenching quick
                     slip-   stream.

From Jericho Pier

In a sea of return everything   cleaves to shore
low waves susurrate   half-bury a woman's
blouse a man's   khaki shorts
though between the clouds   a blue sky flies

refracts the houses' grand windows   up on the hill
where buzz-saws shriek-down   a façade
and build another up   so when the wind
    turns   soaks your cuffs
you make a run for it

    all the way across a broad sweep of sand where a hundred blue
    mussel shells hinge
    open and empty like something just
    flown
    blue birthhouses humming
    with all they no longer hold.

Lives of the Soul

(*with words from poems by Susan McCaslin**)

I find the bright field
    unknowable, illimitable
in the image of a door painted white on the face of a house,
in the face of an infant conceived in rape who shines
on the waters of my memories
    familiar beyond naming
on a morning's city beach where a tree felled
on a mountain escaped its capturing boom,
was carried in tides and now
we may lean against that mountain and rest
    postures of unposturing
find our seat in the saddle of the small brown mare
who waits until we find
the quiet in our hips, gentleness in hands
to ease the cold steel bit
    the body physical, the body soul
    intermingling
as the moon's full mountains turn their headlamps on

*The italicized words are from Susan McCaslin's poems, "Mapping the Human Genomes," "Shanti, Shanti, Shanti," and "Postures of Surrender."

What Is Served

—for Joseph Plaskett

After three months of blowing hard
the Bloodgood Maple's half-bled,
the cars at the curb heaped,
tires steeped
in a bright raw confetti.

Watchers at windows,
walkers in the careless day drink
from its ripeness,
the last leaves like lanterns
far apart
in a late and private garden

what old painters see

after their models, young lovers, leave,
and they make still-lifes
out of tea-pots
and china cups laid out
on a burning vermilion cloth.
An entire plane angled, tipped to pour
into our own bone cups
the blood of trees
as a god feeds a god and we one of these.

A Fine Disorder

On Encountering *Bonheur de Vivre* by Matisse

Joy! all-at-once joy! And sex! saplings! lovers! all of one rhythm
billow-and-curve a beast plundering dei Franceschi and
Cezanne but this is Matisse's explosion of scale his cadmium
crimson golden flesh-pink war on the tyrant Conform and Matisse
our Daimon Sun-Star and now hear *this* voice hoarse and
human coming up through our chest announcing the danger
the rapture the rupture of borrowed and newmade things.

In the Morning When They Fling the Shutters Wide

the cobalt sky, the roofs' green rapture rushes
the unshielded room.

Canvases lean like corpses against the wall,
their bruised fruit stain rags below.
Their silvery leaves. Pleasing. Mere vapours now.

Amélie Matisse and nine-year-old Marguerite
had agreed: he hadn't got to joy,

(seared colour,
poured line—as he used to do),

and though a dealer (coming the next day),
had promised to pay him 400 francs a piece,
they took the still-lifes away.

That night,
all night,
they washed and scraped until
all that remained
was canvas white.

In the morning when they fling the shutters wide
Matisse can see the field of his holy war

atomic ambers, rose madders, sky-dictating
blues stake a blood-claim

the sun calls out with every shameless ray.

From That Night a Fine Disorder was born forty-foot square and scarlet, a great red bird soaring through a blue room and Matisse finally letting the winged line rule, enter where it wished, die where it would, transfusing the whole blue room blood-red, the table at its centre a moving red feast, its far edge lash-thin, its near no edge at all so its patterned cloth floats, floods up the wall in arabesque arcs, and then he tears the fabric of the world again, he slices right through to a hillside where umbrella trees lean broken-spoked to loosen their wedding-white on a green ground so simply drawn, *If I should die* a child's drawing *before I wake* it pierces the polished dream and wakes me to play again.

The Conversation

Matisse stands regimentally correct
in vertically striped blue-and-white pyjamas,
his head held so high
near the top of the painting
he looks like he's drowning
while pretending he's not

while Amélie, opposite,
sits bolt upright
in a black robe, in a blue
chair, but where scar
tissue, jutting
bone should
burden the air between them,
Matisse has painted a garden.

Red fruit and blue pools
echo and proceed
like a recursive code to extend
the eye
to a blue door of horizon
that allows us to let in
an immensity of the same hue
deep-water loved-body blue
that completely surrounds the
sparring pair.

Now we know
Amélie was once the full-bosomed

tree in that garden
(her leaf-green collar and throat),
and the conversation Matisse is having is
not with her, but
with the garden before it's sown,
still part of the floating
blue world that he loves
more than her — more than himself —
so there is no more argument to following
him in, just our
heads above water.

The Conversation, *(1908-1912), by Henri Matisse.*

Even If It Isn't There

Thin
skylights
pink a drab
attic floor
sag a blue ceiling
but they are nothing
to this
end of a room
end of his

rope

Matisse

out of sight
in a far
corner of north
declares he'll
quit. Turns the canvas
away
from himself
abandons his easel, and the black
strap
that ties them together stretches
out
an arrow flying bull's-eye
to a breach
of light staggering through an end

wall surging apricotyellowcream
in the infinite
fullness of summer

trees

A difficult year

1903
from which bursts

his first window

Studio Under the Eaves, *1903, by Henri Matisse*

Shadow, 1905

To recognize at once
what he's never seen before—
the sun giddy with burning
bleaching the sea at Collioure

>so colours must be conceived clotted
>sugar-pink under lavender keels masts
>of tangerine a sky scalloped turquoise-
>violet and pressed almost flat against
>wide French doors flared to the inside
>and so greedy for the light they smear
>the same sea in their glass

In shadowless noon
two shadows—
small pair of kohled windows set high
above the open doors
like an amulet against the Evil Eye or
a cooler view as he reels
from his own fire
in the rays of his instrument.

When Lightning Strikes Only Colours Burn

Everyone knows a wax-winged boy may drown
in the heat of the sea and girls, girls melt too

but always seem whole in the eyes of a boy
whose mother plucked courage
for those wings:

Sunbird *fly* across the divide

through loop-holes to an inside where dusk
wears the purpureus of a woman's

bare arms and all
sorts of desires volt
tekhelet-blue

through the spiralling calm of palm-fronds.

Witness: Artist and Model

Across armchairs or *chaises longues*
young women recline

day-dreamy or alert.

Sometimes their nipples are
outrageously rouged

through gauzy *chemisiers,*

and rosy,
creamy
breasts raised or coyly
concealed, the woman herself

contained in multiple

frames: painting,
shutter,

glass window or door;

a difficult innocence,
the witness of windows, with or without

the features of a face.

The Limits of Windows

"Drawing [the female body], this is how one possesses..."

    Aspasia

               Agnodike

       Theano

                Bonheur

     Morisot

           Villepreux-Power

       Eglui

     Ayrton

         Cassett

               Bracquemond

         Bashkirseff

                      Matisse

Transit

When a room is a window

transparent to itself
when a cyan wall passes through

marble table seat of chair

white ribs of a radiator X-ray
long white sheers to lift
inhalations of light

wash away
whole strips of gold floor

darkest days of the war and unable to serve
Matisse fixes one part of his mind
to solid brown tablebase   black leg of chair
and drifts

through the emptiness of form

a transit of clarity
the feeling of peace

passing through.

The Window, *1916, by Henri Matisse*

Slice, *The Piano Lesson*, 1916

A green triangle seven feet tall

slices through an open window

painting as experiment

in geometric will

played in counterpoint

to the painter's own heart

hidden in vast grey space

hieratic   without face

on high and distant

above a traitor's gate.

The room unsettles

around the eye of a boy

young son captive at a pink piano

half his pink face a triangle too

his mind ticks in time

to the march of the metronome

the child abandoned

even by the female perched

as an angel

Jumble, 1917

Now he remakes the scene
   He jumbles it with comforts
places a woman-helper beside the boy
   sister-helper beside the boy
head of the angel chopped off
   pray no longer to the head of angels!
and in the mind no ticking
   and in the mind music.

Everyone's skin is bronzed
   The sun reliably shines
the older son smokes in a nearby chair
   music curls from his cigarette
the wife rocks beside a fountain's trill
   steady as a rock outside the window
and within
   the loving father?
a softer bigger pinker piano.

   And so it fails?
The terrible tension crowded out
   no metronomic march
no trespass of will
   wire in the instrument
to make us be still, look *again*—
   I will—
at the killing years.

       So the boy's already grown?
and his brother 48-hours from war
           the sons he loves, as you'd have him love you
time's green rush so fleet
           it *should* slice right through
all of the body's windows
           as green as the shadow youth leaves behind
but for the tender captive heart of a father.

The Music Lesson, *1917, by Henri Matisse*

Tilt

—for Christine McDowell

      to the bounty of the table.
      for their return
      and cleanses the palate
      through mint-green windows
      blue sky eases
      room where a cool-
      bold diagonals to a second
     to the ceiling then across
     them almost
     whose spire lifts
     in a domed wire cage
     -leafed and singing
     parakeets gold-
    to a pair of
    of their own interests
    up the odd angles
    stems that carry them
    on almost-invisible
    'blush of poppies sprung
   plump lemons on a patterned cloth
   in to savour
   over its edge to call them
   almost out of its frame
   print of a table that tilts
  at a tacked-to-the-wall cheap
  stare
  and so sometimes unsleeping
  safe
  they are finally
 endeavor to believe
 returned from another country
two women recently
Inside a one-room apartment

Woman Before *Woman Before a Fish Bowl*, 1922

Ragged green body
of a gold-mouthed
fish almost
torpedoes
the private circuit
of my musing.

Henriette*

Silent   grave   Henriette is an eye: She sees

—flicker   trace   turn—
of gold fish in a glass bowl
placed before her and filled
with a liquid
blue-green   glowing as the lattice screens
behind her glow
silent
the same over the one open and the one closed window.

*Henriette Darricarrére was a ballet dancer and musician who was Matisse's model for seven years, during which time she became a close friend to him and his whole family. This poem is based on Woman Before a Fish Bowl, 1922, by Henri Matisse.

Seated Woman, Back Turned

The cement stoop in the front of a little house
my family lived in awhile
where I sat on summer evenings, 14 years old,
bony knees, chest, face warm, still *being*
warmed after the heat of a summer day

all on my own, no one calling or screaming

rooftops and poplars slipped into silhouette,
the rim of the sun caught at the edges of things
as their insides filled with night,
and a horizon
I hadn't really seen before —
just, sort of, abiding —

Matisse made one sky thus:
left-swinging and horizontal,
deliquescent over the silk
and flex of a bay
and the play
of sailboats

this one window so wide to the outside.

Uncaged, 1948

For twenty-five years his paintings tessellate with rugs
screens embroideries as windows disappear. Another war.

Marguerite's captured by the Gestapo escapes from a cattle
car tells her father every detail of her torture.

Years wash away. Then a palm tree looms like a giant's face
in a window-frame cast in intergalactic-black,

blackness rebooted by light evolved inward to snap
the palm fronds pinealian bluegreen yellowblack,

protomythically black as dream-time in which the body
repairs after the horrors of its age. Like a nightsky the curtain

on the right that sparks its own seeds unpainted uncaged
and breeds its fruit black-leafed to hook and eye the dark.

The poems refers to the painting "Interior with Egyptian Curtain," *1948, by Henri Matisse.*

Calling like Prayer (Chapel of the Rosary, 1951)

This whiteness

    if it were in the mind

would terrify

    would double

and double

    until we were

lost

    but doubleness dissolves

in the glass   of seventeen windows
where the sun calls   like prayer
to bathe   white walls
altars   agonies in bright-burning
love-making   yellow rinsed in the
blue   stillness
of sandbars   where even terror
may follow   shifts

of light in the vertical spirit   of windows
though no promise is made   but ease
when solar white flares   through the atmospheres

obliterating idolatries

    as fish will leap and thread
new light across   a lake of windows.

Chapel of the Rosary at Vence was entirely designed by Henri Matisse.

Henriette Darricarrère

—from Figure décorative sur fond ornemental *(1925-1926),*
by Henri Matisse

Matisse, a man as serious as me,
wants my beauty as a bronze *cuirasse*.

I've been with him seven years —
asylum after such a war and work, that dignity.

In the studio, delirium — light floats through Moorish screens,
only the wallpaper poised.

He wears a suit, scandal-proof, and I'm disrobed
but a great power, as you can see, in my uprightness.

Today he paints one side of me shoulder-to-thigh: a slab.
My right side as usual curved and proud

a column against which he breaks the world
into bands of colour.

Today he invents four lemons in a green bowl beside me,
hums a tune A-minor, bee-yellow as clouds

on the wallpaper shout timpanis of red-white flowers
the carpets at my feet bar blue-rust-sage like waves

on a seashore over which I calmly gaze.

We work all day, and tonight, he'll row backwards

across the bay to settle his nerves
while I'll go home to practice my solo

to reassemble my fate.
My ears will ache with stage fright

my fingers stiff on the violin strings
and I'll feel more lonely even than he does

but he's coming for the concerto
and Madame from Paris too

and she'll tell me again about Bohain en Vermandois
where he was raised, where they mock him still,
but the weavers there made a cloth — *firework*
that gave the colour of his rage.

An asylum I can't enter in my upright way
and as these are my final days to learn from him

I must find my own music, or fail,
that dignity.

The First Supper

(*after* Interiéur au Vase Etrusque *by Henri Matisse*)

This is The First Supper. The table laid. This is the First Principle and the woman at the centre its fine-eyed banquet and song. So easily missed the woman so easily mistaken for someone's lover. For the genius in someone else's eye. When I fall asleep so close to her feast laid out on a long black table. So easily missed *this is my body given for thee*. So easily missed the table's blue-blackness that infinitely returns to origin and the womb of the woman even with and equal to its powercord. Its powercord infinitely undulating between lime-bright curves that splash lemon-fruit with lemon-light amidst oranges more themselves because of it, the woman's womb-snake-beast-body *given for thee* to forge the integrity of my place. To seed and shape the womb-snake and shamelessly display straight-up from the plumb-line where a ringing radiant beast-beat dances with the woman in me and the woman in Matisse.

Notes on the Poems

Amy Clampitt, "The Sun Underfoot Among the Sundews," *Staying Alive*, Neil Astley, Editor (New York: Hyperion/Miramax Books, 2003) page 420.

Joy Harjo, "This Morning I Pray for My Enemies," *Conflict Resolution for Holy Beings* (New York: W. W. Norton & Company, 2015).

Attributed to Guatama Buddha, "Luminous, monks, is the mind…" Sutta, Anguttara Nikaya (A.I.8-10), online.

Definitions of *anatta* can be found at "Anatta and the Four Noble Truths," Gil Fronsdal, October 2002, online, and "The Fact of Impermanence," by Piyadassi Thera, online.

Tomas Tranströmer, "After a Long Drought." *The Great Enigma: New Collected Poems* (New York: New Directions Books, 2006), page 138.

In "Theory of Search and Find" the hypothetic experiment is based upon "How to create the quietest place on Earth," Video, *New Scientist* online, Accessed November 20, 2014. The epigraph is by Rumi, "The Unseen Rain," *Unseen Rain, Quatrains of Rumi*, Translated by John Moyne and Coleman Barks (Boulder, CO: Shambhala Publications, 2001) Online.

"The Field Speaks of its Persistence," quotes Wallace Stevens, "Thirteen Ways of Looking at a Blackbird," section VIII. *Wallace Stevens: The Collected Poems* (Vintage Books Edition, 1990), page 94.

The epigraph for "Triolet for Afghanistan" is by Asadulla Habib, "The

Story of My Country." *Language for a New Century, Contemporary Poetry from The Middle East, Asia, and Beyond*, edited by Tina Chang, Nathalie Handal, and Ravi Shankar (New York: W. W. Norton & Co. Inc., 2008), p. 400.

"A Photograph of War, An Najaf," depicts an AP Photo by Jean-Marc Bouju at An Najaf, Iraq. The original caption is no longer online, but a statement at this website reads, "The photo was taken during a rare moment of humanity in a war zone, Bouju said, when a father who had been taken prisoner by American troops was allowed to hold his 4-year-old son." Online.

"The Stoning" is inspired by a collage of the same name by Perry Fletcher Thompson that appeared in *Harper's* magazine, December 2005.

In "Dear Cancer," the phrase "lost to our senses but not perished" is misremembered from "lost to sense, but not perished, not perished," by Marilynne Robinson in *Housekeeping* (New York: HarperPerennial Canada, 1980), page 160.

"Lives of the Soul," contains italicized words from Susan McCaslin's poems, in this order: "Mapping the Human Genomes," *Lifting the Stone* (Hamilton, ON: Seraphim Editions, 2007), 23; "Shanti, Shanti, Shanti," *The Disarmed Heart* (Toronto: The St. Thomas Poetry Series, 2014), 38; "Postures of Surrender," *Lifting the Stone*, 60; and again "Mapping the Human Genomes," *Lifting the Stone,* 23.

The painting referred to in the poem "From that Night a Fine Disorder," is *The Dessert: Harmony in Red, 1908*, by Henri Matisse.

The painting referred to in the poem "Tilt" is *Flowers and Parakeets,* 1924, by Henri Matisse.

The painting that inspired the poem "Seated Woman, Back Turned" is *Seated Woman, Back Turned to Open Window,* 1922, by Henri Matisse.

I am indebted to Hilary Spurling for the extensive research in her biography *The Unknown Matisse, A Life of Henri Matisse: Volume One, 1869-1908* and *Matisse the Master, A Life of Henri Matisse: Volume Two, 1909-1954* (London: Penguin Books, 2005). Spurling's phrase "a fine disorder" appears in my poem "From That Night a Fine Disorder."

Other helpful resources for my Matisse poems were *Bonnard/Matisse: Letters Between Friends 1925-1946* (New York: H.N. Abrams, 1992); exclusively for the 320 colour reproductions, John Elderfield's *Henri Matisse: A Retrospective* (New York: Museum of Modern Art, 1992); *Henri Matisse, Jazz* (New York: George Braziller, 1985) and; "Collecting Matisse and Modern Masters: The Cone Sisters of Baltimore," May 26–September 30, 2012, Vancouver Art Gallery exhibition.

Acknowledgements

I am grateful to the Canada Council for the Arts for a generous grant and the British Columbia Arts Council for a scholarship that supported the writing of some of these poems, and to Luciana Ricciutelli, Editor-in-Chief, and Renée Knapp, Publicist, of Inanna Publications for publishing and promoting this book.

Thank you, dear reader.

Thanks are owed to the editors of the following presses, websites, and publications in which some of these poems first appeared, some in earlier versions: *After You* (2016); *In Fine Form, 2nd edition, A Contemporary Look at Canadian Form Poetry*, edited by Kate Braid and Sandy Shreve, (Halfmoon Bay, BC: Caitlin Press Inc., 2016); *WomenArts Quarterly Journal* (2015; 2016 as Editors' top ten selections from a decade); *Canadian Literature* (2015); *The Limits of Windows* chapbook (North Vancouver, BC: David Zieroth: The Alfred Gustav Press, 2014); *Literary Review of Canada* (2013); *Global Poetry Anthology*, "After Cancer" shortlisted for the 2011 Montreal International Poetry Prize, (Montreal: Vehicule Press, 2011); *FreeFall Magazine* (2010, Third Prize and Honourable Mention in annual poetry prize contest); *The Dalhousie Review* (2010); *Vallum* (2008); *Event 45.2*; *The Antigonish Review*; *The Malahat Review*; *Nashwaak Review* (Vol 24-25).

Very special thanks to members of The Poetry Squad writing workshop, Bibiana Tomasic, Dawn Petten, and Ellen McGinn, excellent companions in writing who became friends for life. Thanks also to the poets in The Compossibles' reading series for the shared discovery of poets around the world. Kate Braid and Bibiana Tomasic offered invaluable reviews of an early draft of the manuscript; editor Harold Rhenisch gave a brilliant crash course in the protean mobility of form; Ann West knew the order; Isabel Huggan of Humber College was a straight-shooting, warm-hearted mentor; Linda Svendsen, Peggy Thompson, and Keith Maillard of the University of British Columbia offered generous encouragement in various genres. Deep gratitude also to most excellent dharma teacher, Michele McDonald, and to light-bearers Christine McDowell, Deborah Prieur, Eva DiCasmirro, and Moira Simpson. Finally, love, love, love to Ronald Martin Grant whose shining intelligence, courage, and tender heart make life more remarkable every day.

Photo: Ron Grant

Leslie Timmins is the author of the chapbook *The Limits of Windows*. Shortlisted for the Montreal International Poetry Prize, winning honours in magazines in Canada and the United States, and published in numerous magazines and anthologies, her poems are strongly influenced by years spent living in Europe and the Canadian Rockies. Activism, a decades-long Vipassana meditation practice, and a varied work life—from waitress to housing advocate to editor—have provided a landing base for her writing. Leslie lives with her husband in Vancouver. See www.PoemsUnlimited.com for further information.